Andy M

The Inspirational Story of Tennis Superstar Andy Murray

Copyright 2015 by Bill Redban - All rights reserved.

This document is geared towards providing exact and reliable information in regards to the topic and issue covered. The publication is sold with the idea that the publisher is not required to render accounting, officially permitted or otherwise, qualified services. If advice is necessary, legal or professional, a practiced individual in the profession should be ordered.

In no way is it legal to reproduce, duplicate, or transmit any part of this document in either electronic means or in printed format. Recording of this publication is strictly prohibited and any storage of this document is not allowed unless with written permission from the publisher. All rights reserved.

The information provided herein is stated to be truthful and consistent, in that any liability, in terms of inattention or otherwise, by any usage or abuse of any policies, processes, or directions contained within is the solitary and utter responsibility of the recipient reader. Under no circumstances will any legal responsibility or blame be held against the publisher for any reparation, damages, or monetary loss due to the information herein, either directly or indirectly.

The information herein is offered for informational purposes solely, and is universal as so. The presentation of the information is without contract or any type of guarantee assurance.

The trademarks that are used are without any consent, and the publication of the trademark is without permission or backing by the trademark owner. All trademarks and brands within this book are for clarifying purposes only and are the owned by the owners themselves, not affiliated with this document.

Table of Contents

Introduction

Chapter 1: Youth & Family Life

Chapter 2: Professional Life

Chapter 3: Personal Adult Life

Chapter 4: Philanthropic/Charitable Acts

Chapter 5: Legacy, Potential & Inspiration

Conclusion

Introduction

As the title already implies, this is a book about [The Inspirational Story of Tennis Superstar Andy Murray] and how he rose from his life in Scotland to become one of today's leading and most-respected tennis players. In his rise to superstardom, Andy has inspired, not only the youth, but fans of all ages throughout the world.

This book also portrays the struggles that Andy had to overcome during his early childhood years and his teen years until he became what he is today. A notable source of inspiration is Andy's service to the community and his strong connection with the fans of the sport. He continues to serve as a relatable, understanding superstar in a sport that certainly needs it.

Combining incredible mental fortitude, impeccable mechanics, an aggressive play style, and high tennis IQ, Andy has shown the ability to completely dominate a match. From being a young boy who dedicated his free time to the tennis court, to becoming one of the greatest tennis players of his generation, you'll learn how this man rose to the ranks of the best players today.

Thanks again for downloading this book. Hopefully you can take some of the examples from Andy's story and apply them to your own life!

Chapter 1:

Youth & Family Life

Andrew Barron Murray was welcomed into the world on May 15th, 1987. Born to father, William, and mother, Judith, in Glasgow, Scotland, Andy was part of an athletic family. His grandfather, Roy Erskine, was a professional level football player during the 1950s. Andy's brother, Jamie, also went on to become a professional tennis player.

Andy experienced a life-altering event when he was only eight years old. While he was sitting in a classroom at Dunblane Primary School, an armed man named Thomas Hamilton broke into the school and shot a total of thirty-two people before shooting himself in the school's gymnasium. Andy and Jamie were both in attendance during the time of the shooting but neither were physically injured.

At the time, Andy was too young to piece together the details of the tragedy, though he was later more candid of his recollection in his autobiography entitled, *Hitting Back*. The community struggled to come to terms with the tragedy at the time, and the event is still considered to be one of the most devastating in the United Kingdom over the past quarter century.

Andy and Jamie were both active children, showing a strong interest in sports, especially tennis. By the time he was twelve years old, Andy entered and won his first big tennis tournament. This victory at the Florida's Orange Bowl showed that Andy certainly had great potential to be a tennis superstar one day.

However, as with most child phenomenon, Andy would still need to put in a great deal of work in order to stay ahead of his peers.

After enrolling at Dunblane High School, Andy was invited to train with the Rangers Football Club. However, he made a bold decision to not join the football club, and instead, turned his focus on fully pursuing a career in tennis. Soon after, he decided to move to Barcelona, Spain and attend the Schiller International School, where he would focus intensely on honing his mechanics and deepening his understanding of the game. He even trained with Emilio Sanchez, who was the world's number one ranked doubles player at one point.

For a teenage boy in high school, the time commitment that Andy gave to his tennis pursuits would be considered a great sacrifice by anyone's standards. However, his countless hours of practice were not without reward. After joining the Futures circuit and Challenger circuit in 2003, Andy showed mental toughness along with elite technical skills. On the court, he appeared to be wise well beyond his years and before long, became ubiquitous in the ranks of junior tennis.

During 2013, Andy was ranked as high as number six in the junior rankings. By the end of 2004, Andy was going deep into most of the tournaments in which he participated. In September of 2004, Andy was victorious in the US Open junior title and was given the prestigious "Young Sports Personality of the Year" award by the BBC. Andy reached the number two position in the junior rankings during 2014. The very next year, Andy became the youngest British player to ever compete in the Davis Cup.

Andy's tennis success during his teenage years did not come without obstacles. At the age of sixteen, he was diagnosed with a bipartite patella, a condition in which the kneecap is separated into two bones rather than being fused. The knee pain that would come and go was certainly enough for many people to call it quits on the dream of becoming a professional athlete. However, Andy decided to accept the cards that he was dealt and move forward with his tennis dreams. Even to this day, Andy can be seen holding his knee during various tennis tournaments and has even been forced to pull out of some events because of it.

There is no doubt that Andy's childhood was one that provided him many sources of motivation and praise, which allowed him to excel in his sport. Whether it was the motivation to beat his older brother or the positive encouragement from his tennis coach, Leon Smith, Andy was always a person who found ways to draw inspiration from his surroundings. He always had a naturally competitive disposition, even as a youth, and tennis was a way for him to channel that energy into a productive means.

Chapter 2:

Professional Life

Andy turned professional in April of 2005 and was awarded a wild card entry in a clay-court tournament called the Open SEAT, which took place in Barcelona. Andy's first professional showing resulted in a loss to Jan Hernych in three sets.

Andy's first ATP match win came against Santiago Ventura, which Andy won in straight sets. He followed this with a second round victory against Taylor Dent, before finally losing to Thomas Johansson in the third round. This impressive performance at Queen's propelled Andy into a wild card position for Wimbledon. As the 312th ranked player in the world, Andy reached the third round of the men's singles tournament. By doing so, he became the first Scot in the Open Era to accomplish such a feat. Andy's third round exit was against David Nalbandian, though he held a two sets to love lead during the match.

Andy kept his momentum rolling by winning two Challenger events, beating the number four ranked player, Marat Safin, in his first Masters event. Then he beat Andrei Pavel in the first round of the US Open after being down two sets to one. Andy participated in the Davis Cup, once again, and was chosen for the opening singles rubbers, though he lost to Stanislas Wawrinka.

Andy's next tennis experience was his biggest yet when he made his first ATP final at the Thailand Open in which he lost in straight sets to Roger Federer, who was the number one ranked player in the world at the time. Andy moved up quite a bit in the rankings during the course of the year, finishing as the sixty-forth ranked player in the world. Additionally, he was named the "Scotland Sports Personality of the Year" for 2005 by the BBC.

Andy competed on the full circuit for the first time during the 2006 season. Despite a disappointing first round defeat at the Australian Open to Gael Monfils, Andy went on to reach the fourth round for the first time in his career at both Wimbledon and the US Open. He played in the Davis Cup, once again, and later went on to defeat Roger Federer in Cincinnati, breaking Federer's fifty-five match winning streak on hard courts. After a loss to Roddick in the late rounds, Andy found himself in the top twenty rankings for the first time in his young career.

Andy found revenge when he defeated Roddick, later that year, in San Jose, California. Soon after, Andy emerged victorious at the SAP Open, beating Lleyton Hewiit, the eleventh ranked player in the world at the time. Lastly, Andy was a finalist in the Legg Mason Tennis Classic in which he played doubles with his brother. Andy suffered an injury in the French Open and finished the year in recovery from back issues and cramps.

The 2007 year was bittersweet for Andy as he suffered his share of setbacks and injuries, though he was now universally regarded as one of the top twenty players in the world and a household name amongst casual tennis fans. In hindsight, the year turned out to be a breakthrough year for Andy. He showed that he could stand across the court with the best players in the world and be a real threat.

Andy's 2007 season featured a coaching change from Brad Gilbert to Miles Maclagan, as well as the hiring of a team of experts that worked with Andy. He reached the fourth round at the Australian Open before losing a five-set match to Rafael Nadal, the second ranked player in the world at the time. He reached the final round in the tournaments at Metz and Doha to finish off the year, and he ended as the eleventh ranked player in the world.

2008 was a roller-coaster year for Andy as he dealt with a first round loss in the Australian Open, followed by a third round loss in the French. However, he bounced back with a quarter-final appearance at Wimbledon, followed by a finals appearance at the US Open. To get to the final round of the US Open, Andy defeated Rafael Nadal, becoming the first Brit since Greg Rusedski to get to the final of a major tournament. Andy lost in straight sets to Roger Federer in the finals, but his popularity was surging at this time due to his superb play.

At the 2008 Olympics in Beijing, Andy dealt with another setback in the form of a poor performance on the global stage against Yen-hsun Lu of Taiwan, the seventy-seventh ranked player in the world. Now a trend in Andy's career, he bounced back, once again, to finish the year strong, winning a handful of tournaments and going deep into some others, including a semifinals appearance in the Masters

Cup. By year's end, Andy was the fourth ranked player in the entire world, and the pressure was starting to build around him.

Andy started the 2009 season just as he finished the 2008 campaign in the form of a victory at the Qatar Open in Doha in which he defeated Roddick in straight sets. Another notable victory came when Andy defeated the world's number one player, Rafael Nadal, in Rotterdam as he earned his eleventh career title.

While dealing with recovery from a virus, Andy was forced to withdraw from Dubai and take some time off. After his return, Andy lost to Nadal in the finals of the Indian Wells tournament, but came back to defeat Novak Djokovic for a Masters title only a week later. After the Monte Carlo Masters, the Rome Masters and Madrid Masters, Andy was ranked as the number three player in the world. This marked the highest ranking that a British male had ever reached in the Open Era.

Another historic victory came at Queen's when Andy defeated James Blake to become the first British winner of the tournament since 1938. Then, Andy emerged victorious in Montreal after an impressive finals victory against Juan Martin del Potro in which he won in three sets. The outstanding tournament performance propelled Andy into the second spot in the world rankings, which he held until the US Open.

Andy dealt with a wrist injury at the US Open, eventually losing in straight sets to Marin Cilic. Andy won both of his singles matches at the Davis Cup but decided afterwards to take some time off to give his injured wrist a little time to heal. After six weeks off from competitive play, Andy came back to win at Valencia.

In 2010, Andy joined Laura Robson to represent Britain in the Hopman Cup where they reached the final round before losing to Spain. In the Australian Open, Andy was able to defeat Nadal and Cilic in superb fashion before losing to Roger Federer, the world's number one at the time, in the final round.

Andy went deep into the BNP Paribas Open followed by first round exits in the Sony Ericsson Open and the Monte-Carlo Rolex Masters. However, Andy's ability to bounce back from lackluster performances shined through once again as he went into the third round at the Rome Masters and made a quarterfinals appearance at the Madrid. Both times, his run was ended by David Ferrer.

Andy had a successful 2010 Wimbledon experience in which he reached the semi-finals before losing to Rafael Nadal in straight sets. Soon after, Andy made the decision to replace his coach, Mike MacIagan, with Alex Corretia. With the season halfway over, Andy regained his focus and got to the final round of the 2010 Farmers Classic before losing to Sam Querrey, who Andy had defeated in their previous four meetings.

Andy, then, defended his Canadian Masters title, becoming the first player to do so since Andre Agassi accomplished the feat fifteen years prior.

The tournament victory sent a statement that Andy was back in dominant form as he defeated Nadal and Federer in straight sets. Furthermore, the tournament victory also ended an eight-month drought for Andy and served as a great confidence boost.

In the Shanghai Rolex Masters, Andy beat Roger Federer in straight sets, once again, and did not drop a single set throughout the entire tournament. This showing marked one of the best in Andy's young career. After a second round loss at the Valencia Open 500, Andy was part of a great family moment as he teamed up with Jamie to win the doubles title - the first in Andy's career.

After a loss to Gael Monfils in the quarterfinals of the BNP Paribas Masters tournament, Andy was moved down to fifth in the world rankings. Andy's 2010 season ended in dramatic fashion as he reached the Tour finals to face Nadal. The match went over three hours and ended in a final set tie-breaker in Nadal's favor.

Andy injured his elbow before the 2011 Barcelona Open Banco Sabadell and was forced to withdraw his name. Soon after, he made it to the semifinals in the Rome Masters where he lost to Novak Djokovic. Andy showcased his talents in two hard-fought battles at the French Open before losing to Nadal in the semifinal round.

Later, in 2011, Andy beat Jo-Wilfried Tsonga to win his second title at Queen's. He continued this hot streak with a superb showing at the 2011 Western & Southern Open in which he defeated Djokovic. Andy emerged victorious in the Thailand Open, and then won his third title in four tournament appearances when he won the Rakuten Japan Open. In the Rakuten Japan Open, Andy won the singles tournament, as well as the doubles tournament, with his brother as his teammate.

To finish off his 2011 campaign, Andy defended his Shanghai Masters title by dominating David Ferrer via straight sets in the final round. Andy moved into fourth place in the world rankings by year's end, although he was recovering from a slight groin pull at the time.

After the switch from Alex Corretia to Ivan Lendi, as his coach, Andy entered the 2012 year with the same momentum that he had built from 2011. A notable match in Andy's career came in the 2012 Australian Open in which Andy made it to the semi-finals to face Djokovic. The match lasted almost five hours and was a beautiful showcase of skill.

Andy's next big accomplishment came in the form of a Wimbledon finals appearance. After defeating Jo-Wilfried Tsonga, Andy lost in the final round to Federer. Despite a disappointing end to the tournament, Andy became the first British male to get to the final round of Wimbledon, since Bunny Austin did it seventy-four years prior.

Andy represented his country in the 2012 Summer Olympics in London when he participated in the singles, mixed doubles and doubles. He teamed with his brother in the doubles tournament, but the duo lost in the first round. In the mixed doubles, Andy and Laura Robson advanced all the way to the finals before losing to the duo from Belarus, taking home a silver medal.

Andy took center stage in the singles, however, dominating the field and finishing the tournament with a victory over Federer in straight sets. In Andy's journey to gold in the singles tournament, he only lost forty-six games and one set in total. Andy's incredible performance in front of the London crowd was something that British sports fans will always remember. Furthermore, he became the first Brit to win the Olympic singles gold in over 100 years.

Andy faced a setback after his Olympic dominance in the form of a knee injury at the Rogers Cup. After retiring early, he took some time off to recover. His first major tournament of the season was the US Open where he won the first two rounds in straight sets. The third and fourth round match-ups against Feliciano Lopez and Milos Raonic, respectively, were hard-fought, and Andy gutted them out in impressive fashion.

The quarterfinals featured a comeback from Andy, who was down a set and two breaks, to defeat Marin Cilic in four sets. The semifinals match against Tomas Berdych went almost four hours before Andy finished it off. The victory over Berdych marked Andy's second straight Grand Slam final appearance, bringing him to the forefront of the sports world. He rode this momentum into the final round, defeating Djokovic in five sets and making him the first Brit to win a Grand Slam final in over seventy-five years, as well as the first Scottish man to win in over a century.

The win at the US Open put Andy in the record books for a few different categories. He became the first male player to win the Olympic gold medal and the US Open in the same year. Andy's victory over Djokovic also was the 100th Grand Slam match victory of his career.

Andy finished the year as the number three ranked player in the world, after hovering around the fourth and fifth spot for the previous couple of years. Additionally, Andy finished in third place in the "Sports Personality of the Year" award by the BBC. He also won the "World Breakthrough Athlete of the Year" at the Laureus World Sports Awards.

Andy won the Brisbane International title in early 2013 by defeating Grigor Dimitrov in the final round via straight sets. After a beautifully played semifinal match against Federer, Andy advanced to the finals of the Australian Open to face Djokovic. For Andy, this marked the third straight final appearance at a Major and the second in a row against Djokovic. Andy eventually lost to Djokovic in four sets, ending the Australian Open as the tournament's runner-up, his third at the event.

After winning the Miami Masters, Andy jumped over Federer in the world rankings, though he briefly fell back into the number three spot after a loss to Wawrinka in Monte Carlo. Andy took some time off after being forced to retire from the Rome Masters, due to a hip injury. He did not take part in the French Open, but he was able to rehabilitate in time for the 2013 Aegon Championships in which he was the top overall seed. Andy won the tournament and then took his third title at Queen's Club only a few weeks later.

Andy was on a roll, heading into Wimbledon, and had not lost a match on grass since the Wimbledon final from the year before. This time around, he defeated Benjamin Becker, Yen-hsun Lu, Tommy Robredo, and Mikhail Youzhny in the first four rounds. Andy's next match-up, against Fernando Verdasco, was a dramatic thriller in which Andy came back from a two set deficit to win in five sets.

Next, Andy defeated Jerzy Janowicz, who had beaten him in their last match-up. After Janowicz took the first set, Andy turned the tables and won the next three sets, earning his second consecutive Wimbledon final appearance and his third straight final appearance against Djokovic. Heading into the match, Djokovic was considered the favorite by most sources. Andy fought valiantly to take Djokovic in straight sets and became the first Scot to win a Wimbledon title, since Harold Mahoney, over a century before. Additionally, the victory extended Andy's grass court winning streak to eighteen matches.

After the 2013 Davis Cup, Andy decided to end his season prematurely, so he could undergo surgery to fix his lower back issues. The pain had been lingering for many months and he decided to give it his full attention, rather than allowing it to continue to flare up randomly. The 2013 season was another stepping stone in Andy's career, as he was named the prestigious "Sport Personality of the Year" by the BBC.

Chapter 3:

Personal Adult Life

Andy is certainly one of the most relatable athletes in all of tennis, whether it be his down-to-earth personality, or his great ability to connect with the fans of the sport. Because he was born and raised in Scotland, Andy will always have to deal with the never-ending debate regarding his Scottish or British nationality. His nationality is always a topic of discussion and probably will be for the rest of his career, whether it be the media or the general public.

Andy has been in a relationship with Kim Sears, the daughter of former player and current coach, Nigel Sears. Kim is often seen in attendance at Andy's matches and has been one of his biggest supporters throughout his career.

Andy was awarded the Freedom of Stirling award in early 2014, as well as given a Doctor of the University of Stirling. The awards were given to him as a tribute to his great accomplishments and services to the sport of tennis. Additionally, Andy was given the Officer of the Order of the British Empire award as a recognition for his impact on the sport of tennis.

Andy has always been a relatively lanky athlete, but he has put on some muscle during his maturation as a professional. One of the foods that he credits helping him put on some of that lean mass is sushi. Whether it be a post-match dinner or a random lunch in the off-season, Andy loves to load up on the Japanese delicacy.

Andy has been with Adidas since 2009 when he signed a five-year deal with the sportswear giant. Before this, Andy wore Fred Perry on court. His shirt sponsors include the Royal Bank of Scotland, Highland Spring, as well as Shiatzy Chen. For his racket, Andy has chosen to partner with Head, even appearing in advertisements for the company. Andy's most recent endorsement includes teaming up with Rado, the Swiss watch maker, in mid-2012.

Chapter 4:

Philanthropic/Charitable Acts

One of the things that makes Andy such a great role model for the world is that he has made it a point to use his public fame to make a positive impact in society. Andy was a founding member of the "Malaria No More UK" Leadership Council. He helped to launch the charity in 2009, along with David Beckham.

One of the campaigns from the organization was called "Nets Needed" in which Andy made a public service announcement to raise awareness and collect funds in the fight against malaria. Along with his personal and monetary endorsements, Andy has also been very physically involved in events to help the cause, including playing in several different charity events over the years.

A notable event was the "Rally for Relief" charity tennis tournament in which Roger Federer, Novak Djokovic, and Rafael Nadal joined Andy to make the event a major financial and social success. Much of the funds raised through Rally for Relief went to help the flood victims in Queensland.

In 2013, Andy joined Tim Henman to participate in a charity doubles match against Andy's then-coach, Ivan Lendi, and Tomas Berdych in Queen's Club. The funds raised went to help the Royal Marsden Cancer Charity. The event was especially significant to Andy because his best friend, Ross Hutchins, had been diagnosed with Hodgkin's Lymphoma. In addition to putting on a show at the charity event, Andy donated his entire prize money pot from his victory at the AEGON Championships to the charity.

Even though Andy is only in his mid-twenties, he is certainly wise and compassionate beyond his years. His desire to help and give back to the community through multiple avenues shows that he is a very humble star. Additionally, his story shows that we do not need to wait to make it big before we give back, as he started in this journey in 2009, before he was considered one of the top four tennis players in the world - something from which we can all learn.

Chapter 5:

Legacy, Potential & Inspiration

As a player profile, Andy is one of the best ground-strokers in all of the sport, rarely making errors, as he shows an innate ability to anticipate the placement and reactions of this opponents' shots. He is certainly a very athletic player with a unique ability to change direction and alter from offense to defense. This keeps his opponents on edge, as he can hit winners from seemingly anywhere on the court.

Andy's two-handed backhand shot is one of the deadliest that the sport has ever seen, clearly something into which he puts a great deal of work. No matter how much his opponents prepare for it, Andy always seems to be a step ahead. Last, Andy has an elite lob that keeps his opponents off-balance. In addition to his ability to place the lob, he uses the shot at times that his opponents do not expect it.

While his athletic ability is obvious, one of the greatest compliments that one can receive in the sport of tennis is to be called "intelligent." Andy certainly falls into this category. Whether his anticipation, his tactical ability to keep a defender in constant reaction, or the immaculate placement of his backhand shots, Andy's mental understanding of the game is something to be admired. As with all tennis players, Andy performs better on some courts than others. He is best on the fast surfaces, especially grass, but has come a long way in his clay court game - a sign that he is not satisfied with his current level of greatness.

It is debatable whether Andy is playing in the most competitive era that tennis has ever seen. Everyone has their biases, including the "experts" in the sport, but there is no doubt that these last ten years have featured some of the greatest stars that the sport has witnessed. Rafael Nadal, Roger Federer, Novak Djokovic, and Andy Murray, fondly referred to as the "The Big Four", all may have won more titles if they played in a less competitive era. However, watching these great players is so fun because of the fact that they push each other to reach new heights in every single tournament, ultimately raising the level of competition.

Nonetheless, as tennis fans, we are truly blessed to be able to watch the competitiveness of the sport at this current time. Because Andy has been in the public eye for so long, fans often forget that he is still fairly young in his career. He has dealt with public scrutiny incredibly well for a man of such youth, and his future looks even brighter than his past.

Conclusion

I hope this book was able to help you gain inspiration from the life of Andy Murray, one of the best tennis players in the world.

Andy serves as a great representative for Scotland, the United Kingdom, and the sport of tennis. His respectful demeanor and understanding of the legends before him make it very hard for someone to dislike him. Additionally, he is able to keep fans glued to the television, because they know any time he plays in a competition, there is a possibility that he will make history.

Andy has inspired so many people, because he is the star who never fails to connect with fans and give back to the less fortunate. Noted for his ability to dominate the competition on any day, he is a joy to watch on the court. Last but not least, he's remarkable for remaining simple and firm with his principles, in spite of his immense popularity.

Hopefully you've learned some great things about Andy in this book and are able to apply some of the lessons that you've learned to your own life! Good luck in your own journey!

Other Athlete Stories That Will Inspire You!

Miguel Cabrera

http://www.amazon.com/dp/B00HKG3G1W

Babe Ruth

http://www.amazon.com/dp/B00IS2YB48

Buster Posey

http://www.amazon.com/dp/B00KP11V9S

Lou Gehrig

http://www.amazon.com/dp/B00KOZMONW

Mike Trout

http://www.amazon.com/dp/B00HKKCNNU

Anderson Silva

http://www.amazon.com/dp/B00HLBOVVU

Inspirational Football Stories!

Peyton Manning

http://www.amazon.com/dp/B00HJUYTCY

Tom Brady

http://www.amazon.com/dp/B00HJYQTRS

Aaron Rodgers

http://www.amazon.com/dp/B00HJUEDEI

Colin Kaepernick

http://www.amazon.com/dp/B00IRHHABU

Russell Wilson

http://www.amazon.com/dp/B00HK909C8

Calvin Johnson

http://www.amazon.com/dp/B00HJK0YS2

Inspirational Basketball Stories!

Stephen Curry

http://www.amazon.com/dp/B00HH9QU1A

Derrick Rose

http://www.amazon.com/dp/B00HH1BE82

Blake Griffin

http://www.amazon.com/dp/B00INNVVIG

Carmelo Anthony

http://www.amazon.com/dp/B00HH9L3P8

Chris Paul

http://www.amazon.com/dp/B00HIZXMSW

Paul George

http://www.amazon.com/dp/B00IN3YIVI

Dirk Nowitzki

http://www.amazon.com/dp/B00HRVPD9I

Kevin Durant

http://www.amazon.com/dp/B00HIKDK34

Printed in Great Britain
by Amazon